T0095428

AUTO
EDUCATION
FOR
BLING-BLING
WOMEN

DESTINY SIMON

ARCHWAY
PUBLISHING

Archway Publishing books may be ordered through booksellers or by contacting:

Archway Publishing
1663 Liberty Drive
Bloomington, IN 47403
www.archwaypublishing.com
1 (888) 242-5904

Because of the dynamic nature of the Internet, any web addresses or links contained in this book may have changed since publication and may no longer be valid. The views expressed in this work are solely those of the author and do not necessarily reflect the views of the publisher, and the publisher hereby disclaims any responsibility for them.

Any people depicted in stock imagery provided by Getty Images are models, and such images are being used for illustrative purposes only. Certain stock imagery © Getty Images.

ISBN: 978-1-4808-7698-9 (sc)
ISBN: 978-1-4808-7842-6 (e)

Library of Congress Control Number: 2019906483

Print information available on the last page.

Archway Publishing rev. date: 06/11/2019

Contents

Introduction

Thank you for purchasing my book. This journey has been long and hard but worth it. I want to share with women—future friends—things I learned that can help to make your life with your car better.

I served in the US Air Force for eight and a half years, and my job was fixing engines. I was first trained in refrigeration and air-conditioning mechanics. Then I was trained as a diesel mechanic for nuclear missiles.

Growing up, I watched my dad and uncle repair all types of cars. So I know a little about fixing cars. I enjoy helping my friends repair their cars, including educating them on what the issues are. And I want to help you. My goal is for you to learn enough from my book that you feel confident when speaking to the shops about what you need for your car. I want you to know when mechanics are upselling you or when you need something more than what they are offering. The education you receive from this book will help you to find a garage, tire store, and auto-parts store where you can feel safe knowing that you understand what they are saying. Remember that not all parts stores are alike. Some have great customer service and knowledgeable staff, but some don't. So find the one that will fit you. Once you do that, your life with your car will get better.

1
Coolant

How important is water to your body? A car's coolant is basically of the same importance as water is to the human body. Coolant keeps your engine running at the correct temperature. In our cars we use a combination of water and antifreeze. The antifreeze helps to keep your engine cool in high-temp areas and keep the water from freezing in cold areas.

When our cars are running, the parts move up and down. The high speeds at which these mechanical parts move produces friction, which produces heat. To counter that high temperature, a tubular system containing coolant runs through your engine. The coolant absorbs the heat coming off the moving parts so that your engine stays at the desired temperature.

If for some reason you don't have coolant in those tubes, your engine will overheat and quit working. If an extensive amount of damage is done, you will have to replace the whole engine.

Always make sure that you have enough coolant in the plastic reservoir. Make sure you only fill to the line reading "Full." You should not have to fill your reservoir very often. If you are doing so every couple of weeks, then you may have a leak in the reservoir. The heat can cause the plastic to crack.

Or sometimes the hose that runs to the radiator gets old.

If you see water on the ground under the front end of your car, check its color. If it's green, it's your coolant from the radiator and needs to be looked at right away. You can take it to the auto-parts store, and they can show you where the problem is and how you can fix it yourself. Or you can take it to the shop. If you go to the auto-parts store first, you can go to the auto mechanic with knowledge of what's wrong with your car.

It's important to become familiar with the temperature gauge on your dash. When you start your engine, the gauge should read "Cold." When the engine heats up, you'll see the gauge go up about halfway, which is normal. If your gauge has numbers, it should rise to 220 degrees. It should not go above that when you're driving. If it does go past where it normally sits when you're driving, pull in to a gas station or auto-parts store because it's overheating. And because of all those moving parts, you don't have a lot of time before this gets really hot and your engine suddenly stops. Then you have big expensive engine problems.

Remember the people at auto-parts stores are your friends. They will help you diagnose issues.

NOTES

2

Air-Conditioning

Air-conditioning. Oh, how we love the AC in our cars. But that doesn't mean it loves us.

Your car's air conditioner is like your home air conditioner. They both work on a sealed system, meaning that the refrigerant gas inside the tubes will not leak out or be depleted.

When you get your new car, the AC works great. But after about five years, you notice your AC just doesn't blow as cold as it used to. What most people don't realize is that the bumping and shaking of the car engine and the extreme heat or cold will cause problems for your AC. The tubes and connections get old and loose, and the Freon or other refrigerant gas starts to leak out. When that happens, your AC will not blow cold air as it should.

So here's what you do. Go to the auto-parts store, and tell them your AC is not blowing cold air like it used to. They will look at your AC and tell you if you're low on your gas, and if so, they'll tell you which refrigerant gas you need to buy. They will also show you the kit that you will need to purchase. It will come with gauges and a bottle of refrigerant.

Don't let that scare you. This kit is made for beginners, and many auto-parts stores will show you how to hook it up. It's that easy. The handyman whom you use for your home repair may also be able to do it for you if you'd rather not. If you don't have someone like that, ask a friend if her husband or someone she knows can help. It really is easy, and most will not mind helping.

While you're adding the refrigerant, you can include a can of stop leak for your AC. It can fix small leaks. You can also purchase a can of dye that will show you where the leak is.

This is not a total fix for your AC unit, but it could buy you a couple of years before you must take it to a shop and have the whole system fixed.

If you must put refrigerant in your system more than once or twice in six months, you need to have an air-conditioning shop look at it. This shop will diagnose the problem, including checking for leaks, as I mentioned earlier. Hopefully they can fix it. If so, they will put it on a vacuum machine and then put new refrigerant back into the system.

Make sure to question the replacement of parts, and get two or three quotes. Take the quotes to the auto-parts store, and even though they're probably not mechanics, you can ask them questions and see what they think. They deal with this stuff every day and have a lot of hands-on knowledge, so they can help you make the wisest decision.

NOTES

3
Oil

Oil—how important is it? It's kind of like the blood in our bodies. If we don't have it, we die. It's the same with your engine; no oil, and your engine dies. When I first got into auto mechanics, I didn't understand the importance of oil and what it did. Now, having worked for years as a mechanic, I've been educated, and I want to share that knowledge with you.

With all the moving parts in our engines, we normally don't think about what makes them move or how the oil is a big part of why they move. Without oil moving through the engine, the parts that need to move will not move. That's why it's so important not only to have the proper amount of oil in your engine but to change the oil often as well. Most car manuals say to change your oil at three thousand miles and at five thousand miles for newer cars. But considering how important the oil is, I change mine every three thousand miles.

When you change the oil, it's like changing your water filter; you can't see the contaminates, but you know they are there. The filter collects the contaminates from the water. The same is true with the oil. An oil filter strains the oil as the car runs.

During an oil change, old oil is drained and the old filter removed, and new oil and a new are filter put in. If your car could get up and dance when you gave it an oil change, it would.

There are different types of oil available for your engine. What type you use is up to you. Most new cars use full synthetic. What this oil does and its quality can't be beat.

There are four types of oil: synthetic, synthetic blend, high-mileage, and conventional. Each oil has a different purpose.

Full synthetic oil will extend the life of your car by giving extra slickness. It is also the best if you live in an area that is extremely hot in the summer or extremely cold in the winter. In addition, it does not clog your engine and will not build up in to a mud-like texture with age as some other types can do.

Synthetic blend is like full synthetic, just a little bit cheaper. It's a mixture of synthetic and conventional oils and is excellent in cold weather.

High-mileage oil is made for cars with seventy-five thousand miles or more. It has unique additives, and the way it's made helps reduce oil burn-off and to reduce oil leaks that happen in older engines.

Conventional oil is recommended for old cars and moderate driving.

The biggest difference between synthetic oil and traditional oil is the levels of refinement. Both synthetic oil and traditional motor oil are made from refined oil. Most synthetics begin with highly refined crude oil pumped from deep in the ground, the same source as conventional oil. Other synthetic oils are artificially made. It is better ecologically as it produces fewer omissions. It's more expensive, but it's also a better oil. Never run your car when it is low on oil. It will ruin your engine.

I have now given you more information about your car's oil than you'll ever need to know.

NOTES

4
Transmissions

Why do I need a transmission? The transmission is what makes your car move forward and backward. The transmission is kind of like a bicycle. A chain is on the gears, and when you pedal, your bicycle goes forward. If that chain breaks, you can pedal all you want, but you're not going anywhere. And when your transmission breaks, you're not going anywhere.

So let's concentrate on how to take care of your transmission. The number one thing that you can do to extend the life of your transmission is change your transmission fluid every year. It's as simple as that. That is the norm for everyday driving. If you're pulling a trailer, do a lot of racing, or drive in a lot of stop-and-go traffic, you need to check on your transmission every three months. Not necessarily to change the fluid but to check the fluid level. Take your car over to the auto-parts store, and they will show you where the dipstick is and how to check it. You also want to check for floaters and clarity.

Transmission fluid is dyed pink or red. If for some reason it is a dark color, almost black, and you can see something in it, like little pieces of shiny, glitter-like stuff, you could have a problem with your transmission, and you need to get it checked ASAP. Besides that, there isn't much you can do.

If you have a really old car, there are additives you can put in it to make the gaskets swell and stop leaks but only if you're stopping the leak because it's just an old car that you're using until it dies.

NOTES

NOTES

5

Tires

If tires look good on the rims, what difference does it make what they are? Plenty.

When I researched this book, I knew tires were important, but the materials they used, where the products come from, and how they are made are mind-boggling, so enjoy the condensed version.

Tires are made of different layers of rubber. Each layer has a different function.

1. Tire Belts

Rubber-coated layers of steel, crisscrossing at angles, hold the belts in place. Belts provide resistance to punctures and help treads stay flat and in contact with the road.

2. Tire Sipes

Sipes are special treads within the primary tread that improve traction on wet, dirty, sandy, or snowy road surfaces. This is the design you see when you look at the tire.

3. Tire Tread

The tread is the portion of the tire that meets the road. This part is what you pay extra for; the thicker the tire tread, the more expense it is.

4. Tire Grooves

The spaces between two adjacent tread ribs are called tire grooves or tread grooves. They allow water to escape effectively. If they didn't have these spaces, you could hydroplane and slide off the road when it rained or snowed.

5. Tire Shoulder

The outer edge of the tread that wraps into the sidewall area is called the tire shoulder.

6. Tire Sidewall

The sidewall of the tire protects cord plies and features tire markings and information such as the tire's size and type. If you get a nail into the sidewall, by law, you must replace the tire. You cannot plug the hole safely.

7. Tire Inner Liner

This is the innermost layer of a tubeless tire that prevents air from penetrating the tire. In the past, tires had inner tubes, like you do on your bike.

8. Tire Bead

The tire bead is a rubber-coated loop of high-strength steel cable that allows a tire to stay seated on a rim. It works kind of like a rubber band.

9. Tire Body Plies

This is the tire itself, which is made up of several layers of plies. Plies, like polyester cord, run perpendicular to the tire's tread. They are coated with rubber to help bond with other plies and belts to seal in air. Plies give tires strength and resistance to road damage.

Some fun information. They use antioxidants and antiaging products in your tires. Why? Sun, water, and heat destroy the rubber, so to counter that damage, tire companies use antiaging products to make them last longer. Kind of like the cream we use on our faces!

Why are some tires more expensive than others? It's like buying a knockoff purse or the real thing. They're both good, but one is better.

Before you buy new tires, look at your old ones for the wear. Check to see whether the tire wear is the same across the whole tire. If the rubber seems to be thinner on the outside of your tire, you need a front alignment or tie-rod. If the wearing is more in the middle of your tire, you have too much air.

If your steering wheel shakes when you get over thirty miles per hour, it could be because your tires are unbalanced. That often happens when you hit a curb. You lose a little metal strip that is inserted between the tire and rim for balancing. You can usually stop at a tire store and tell them what the symptoms are, and they will diagnose for free. There will be a charge to replace the balancing strip.

If you have the money when you buy tires, get the ones that will last a hundred thousand miles. Then you won't have to worry about tires for a long time. But if you don't have a lot of money, buy the least-expensive ones that go about twenty thousand miles. And if you're really having issues, there are tire shops where you can get decent and inexpensive used tires. They take tires off wrecked cars that still have good tread and are not damaged by the wreck. I had to do that for many years when I was raising my son alone.

Junkyards also have amazing finds. They are not like ones in old movies, with men in dirty T-shirts spitting tobacco. They are big business now and computerized. If you need a new side window or motor for that window, go up to the counter and give them the make, model, and VIN (vehicle identification number) of your car, and they will tell you whether they have it. And they guarantee all parts. But like auto-parts stores, not all junkyards are the same.

NOTES

6

Battery

What does your car battery do? When you push the button or turn the key to start your car, you're sending a message to the battery to send electricity to the starter to start your car. That's why your battery needs to be kept clean and in working order. When you look at the top of the battery, you see two metal prongs that come out of the top or the side of the battery, where two thick wires are attached. That's where you will see white corrosion. Go to the auto-parts store and tell the person you need new battery pads and cleaner for your battery posts.

As far as the cleaner, you can even use Coca-Cola, a baking soda-and-water mixture, or something premade from the auto-parts store. Mix the baking soda or the premix together like a paste, and paint it on the metal posts. Note that it's going to bubble and fizz. When it stops fizzing, take some water and rinse off the residue. Make sure you watch where the water goes. It will go down into the pan or other stuff, and you need to rinse it off. It's actually acid, and if left to dry, it will eat through the wires.

If your battery posts are really corroded, those thick wires that are attached to your battery cable need to be taken off and cleaned underneath the attachment.

Now, you may think that won't stop my car from starting, but yes it will. Your car battery is like ones we put in the TV remote. If there is a small piece of paper between the connections, it will not work. It's the same with your car battery and corrosion. So keep your battery connections and battery clean.

As for maintaining your battery, you can take your car to either an auto-parts store or a big-box store that sells batteries. Ask them how you can check your battery to make sure the water is at the correct level because it evaporates naturally. If you want to pay for someone to clean your battery, a car battery shop will do it.

Another thing you need to look at is the size of your battery, but not the physical size. Unlike regular batteries we use for flashlights, our car batteries on the inside are made with a little amount of electricity to a large amount. This makes a difference with weather and what you're starting. So if you live in an area with extreme weather conditions, you need higher cranking amps. With the correct cranking amps, when you push the button or turn the key, the vehicle starts right up. But if you don't have enough cranking amps, your vehicle may not start the first time, or it may not start at all because of extreme weather conditions.

New cars come with a factory battery, which is not always the best. So if you're in Arizona, South Dakota, or someplace where you have weather extremes, you need to upgrade your battery.

Does it hurt your battery to give somebody a jump? Not if done correctly. The battery cables are color coded. First, put the red clip on the battery's red post. Then hook the black clip to the black post. Do it in the right order, and it won't hurt your battery.

One caution: Never stand directly over a battery when you're giving a jump. Depending on the age of the battery, it can explode.

How long should your battery last? Three to five years, but it depends on where you live. For replacement, go to the auto-parts store to buy a battery; some big-box stores have them as well. Most places will install it for free. Big-box stores give a warranty, so if it dies in year 2, they replace it for free.

NOTES

NOTES

7

Engines

Did you ever wonder how your car works? No, me neither. I just want it to work! So as a woman mechanic, let me explain to you how this works. When you push the button or turn the key, a message is sent to the brain of the engine to start. The brain sends a message to the many sensors that send out gas and electricity to different parts of the engine. A spark is created in the engine, the pistons go up and down, and a very small explosion happens. And voilà, it starts. Those are the basics. A car can come with four cylinders, six cylinders, or eight cylinders.

What does that mean? It has to do with power. Four cylinders will get you good gas mileage, and you can go a hundred miles an hour on the freeway. Six cylinders will get you okay gas mileage, but your power increases and takeoff is good. Eight cylinders do not make for the greatest gas mileage, but this type of car will get you so much power that you leave everybody in the dust. That's why most sports cars have eight cylinders. Of course, some cars are made with turbos, which is just an addition to the engine to increase the power. You can have a four-cylinder engine with a turbo that can go almost as fast as eight cylinders. So before you go out and buy a vehicle, think about how many cylinders you want.

NOTES

NOTES

8

Belts

Why do we have belts in our car? Are they important?

Yes, and you will have to have them change periodically. You can have up to three or four belts in your car engine, and any of them can break at any time. And when they do, you have a major problem. Some of the belts are drive belts, V-belts, timing belts, and a serpentine belt. You also have the belts for your radiator. and some cars have alternator belts.

The serpentine belt is on newer cars. It runs everything, so if that breaks, your car will not run, period. What causes it to break? Heat, cold, and age. There's nothing we can do to stop it, so check your belts every six months.

How do you check your belts? Go to the auto-parts store and look at a new belt on the wall. Then look at the one in your car. If there's a big difference, you need to change it. Age causes them to crack and come apart.

You're probably wondering, *Why do I need to check them in the winter?* Well, cold is just as damaging as heat. Sad to say there is no spring break on caring for the car.

Most of the time, these are things we cannot change ourselves. You can buy the belts ahead of time at the auto-parts store. You can ask the auto-parts people if they know someone who can put the belts on for you. It does not have to be a major hit for your pocketbook.

If the serpentine belt is getting old, it will start squealing when you start the engine or take off fast. That means you need to change it. And that is an expense, but there is no choice on that. You need to take it to an auto repair shop because the engine has to be opened. Kind of like open heart surgery, everything is exposed, and you want the best mechanic to do that.

When it comes to timing belts/timing chains, most likely you will not see your timing belt be-cause it is inside the engine. For most new cars, it is suggested that it be changed between sixty thousand and ninety thousand miles. It is a little pricey, but if you don't change it and it breaks, it can tear up the inside of your engine. When that belts snaps, it flops and hits and snaps all kinds of things, potentially doing thousands of dollars of damage.

NOTES

9

Brakes

The braking system consists of brakes, brake pads, brake fluid, and rotors. I have changed the brake pads and rotors myself. If you really want to learn, it's not hard, and you may be able to borrow the tools from the auto-parts store. To learn to do it, just watch a YouTube video. Be warned you will get dirty.

When your brakes are working well, when you press down on the brake pedal, your car stops nice and smooth, without any grinding noise or jerking. Pressing the pedal causes a multitude of things to happen. It causes brake fluid to be pushed to another area of the brake system, which causes the brake pads to press against the rotor.

This is why you need to make sure you have plenty of brake fluid. Normally, you won't have to add any, but you probably will if you have an old car. The container that holds the brake fluid is usually in the engine compartment, by the windshield. If you go to an auto-parts store, they will show you where it's at. There is a little dipstick to check the fluid level. Adding fluid is simple. Just pour it in until you reach the full line.

There will be times when you have to change your brake pads. Not too often, perhaps once a year, depending on how you drive. The brake pads remind me of a nail file. You use it a little bit, and then you notice is not good anymore because you've scraped off all the stuff that causes it to work. Same thing with brake pads. Every time you put your foot on the brake, you scrape off a little bit of the stuff that makes the pads work.

And like a nail file, some brake pads are better than others. There are four types of brake pads that you can buy. There are expensive ones and inexpensive ones. The difference is how long they last. The most expensive ones are called ceramic brake pads; the least expensive ones are semimetallic. You don't have to use the same type of pads every time you change them. And because they're so easy to change, I normally have my cheap shop change them. I've used the most expensive ones, and what I like about them is they last so long. The choice is up to you. Be aware that the inexpensive ones have a tendency to squeak. But I have used them many times because they are less expensive.

As far as your rotors, they'll often want to change them when having the pads replaced. But you can usually get another one or two uses out of them before you have to change them. You can ask them to flip the rotors.

The rotors are what your brake pads press against to stop your car. Sometimes your rotors get grooves in them, and this will cause your brake pads to wear unevenly, and you won't get as much use out of the pads if the rotors are grooved. If you have worn down your pads to the point that they are grinding, the little screws in the brake pads are scraping your rotors, and the longer you let that go on, the worse it gets. It's also a safety device to tell you to change because soon you will have no brakes. Always remember that if your brakes quit working, pull your emergency brake. It can stop you.

NOTES

10

Windshield Wiper Blades and the Windshield

The type of windshield wiper blades you need depends on where you live. In high-temperature areas, inexpensive blades are fine, but you will have to replace them twice a year, as the heat will destroy the rubber. The auto-parts store will put them on for free.

If you live in a snowy area, you'll need to get the triple blade, which are more expensive. Again, the auto-parts store will put them on for you.

How many times has a stupid rock flown up and put in nick in your windshield? If you go to the auto-parts store right away, you can pick up some stuff like liquid glass to put in that hole so it doesn't crack all the way across the windshield.

Once you get that crack all the way across the windshield, you must replace it. Some of us have windshield insurance, so replacement is free. Some states, like where I live in Texas, you can't get windshield insurance. So what do you do if you can't get that insurance and need to replace your windshield? Go to the junkyard. Many sell used windshields for your car. I love these places; they remind me of treasure hunting. The junkyard will likely know someone who can put it in for you. That's the easiest way to get your windshield changed without it costing a whole lot of money.

The importance of having a windshield that does not have a crack could be the life of your loved one, so change it. I had an experience where an eighteen-wheeler lost part of its load and hit my windshield. The week before, I'd had my windshield changed because of a severe crack. I cannot tell you how thankful I was that I had changed it.

NOTES

NOTES

11

Help, My Service Light Is On

How many times have we seen the Check Engine light and it's given us heart palpitations? What do we do?

Don't panic. One of the first things to do is check to see whether you have a loose gas cap. Always make sure that it's on tight because one that isn't can cause your Check Engine light to go on.

It's usually not an emergency when the light comes on, but that being said, check all your gauges. Make sure that your engine is not over-heating. Make sure your battery-charging indicator is at its normal level. And if you have a newer car, scroll through all your diagnostics. If you don't see anything out of the ordinary, head over to your auto-parts store in the next couple of days, and ask them to hook it up to the computer and see what it says. If they can't find a problem, go to your dealership because this is a dealership issue.

Don't panic when tire-pressure lights come on. These lights are so sensitive that they come on with just one pound of pressure difference. That is not a flat tire. If you see a difference of five pounds, you could have a problem, like maybe a nail, so go by one of the tire stores. They will check for free most of the time.

And if money is tight and you get a nail in the sidewall of your tire, a big-box store will not plug it but will want you to get a new tire. But small tire-repair shops have different ideas, so always check them before you buy.

You should become very familiar with your temperature gauge. It's cold when you start your car and will get up to about 220 degrees when it's warm, and that's where it should stay. If the gauge starts moving upward, your car is overheating and you need to pull off the road, turn on your heater, and see if the temperature goes down. If it does, leave the heater on, and you might be able to drive to the next gas station before turning off your car. You must remember that if the engine overheats too much, it can kill your engine.

Some of the first things to look at if you've got a problem with your water temperature is a water hose, which is located in the front part of your engine. If when you lift the hood steam and water are blowing everywhere, it's most likely the hose, which doesn't cost a lot to fix. You can usually buy the hose, and the auto-parts-store person will show you how to put it on. Know this: you cannot drive your car without coolant/water.

When you check your belts for wear and age, always check your water hoses as well. With the engine off and cool, look at the hoses. Then squeeze all your hoses, one at a time. They should be firm to hard. If you squeeze a hose and it's mushy, like cooked spaghetti noodles, you need to change the hose so that you don't end up on the side of the road.

And make sure that there is nothing blocking the air coming through the front of the radiator. Plastic bags sometimes get sucked into the radiator. Also look at your radiator belt and make sure it's still there. Sometimes when they break, they fly off. If it's gone, you need a tow truck. You cannot drive it far, because your engine will overheat and seize. Then you'll need a new engine.

If your temperature gauge goes up and there doesn't seem to be any problems with your water/coolant, check your oil. If we hit a speed bump too hard, we can crack the oil pan and not know it. As you drive, you leak oil from the pan, which will cause overheating because of the friction caused by the moving parts. So make sure you have oil.

There you go. I wish I could answer your questions directly, but I hope this helps you for now. Happy driving.

NOTES

NOTES

About the Author

 As a sergeant in the United States Air Force, my last job was Diesel Mechanic for the Minuteman missile, and then I trained and became a Refrigeration and Air-conditioning mechanic.

I've always enjoyed working with my hands I enjoy learning how things work which has helped me become a good mechanic.

I wrote this book to help my friends when I'm not available as I'm always the go-to for car problems.

Most of my girlfriends were divorced or single with children and income was a challenge so repairing their cars would cause stress getting it fixed.

My friends knew that I could tell them what was wrong with the car and if I could I would fix it for them. Like when the Air-Conditioning doesn't blow cold air or something is leaking under their car. I didn't mind helping I enjoy doing it and I would like to help you. I wish I could come to your house and look at your car, and tell you what's wrong with it but I can't so I wrote this book so that I could be your girlfriend and help you with your car.

Just because we're bling-bling women doesn't mean we have to be uneducated about our cars.